Transportation

JULIAN ROWE

RIGBY
INTERACTIVE
LIBRARY

Interiors designed by **AMR**
Illustrations by Art Construction
Printed in the United Kingdom

00 99 98 97 96
10 9 8 7 6 5 4 3 2 1

Library of Congress Cataloging-in Publication Data
Rowe, Julian.
     Transportation / Julian Rowe.
        p. cm. – (Science encounters)
     Includes index.
     Summary: Uses familiar examples to explain the scientific
 principles of transportation, covering such aspects as cars, high speed trains, jets, and space
travel.
     ISBN 1-57572-087-6
     1. Transportation – Juvenile literature. [1. Transportation.]
     I. Title. II. Series.
TA1149.R69 1997   96-27560
629.04–dc20   CIP

Acknowledgments
The publisher would like to thank the following for permission to reproduce photographs.

Trevor Clifford, p. 5 (top); Action-Plus, p. 5 (bottom); Mary Evans Picture Library, p .6
(bottom), p. 21 (top); Associated Press/Topham, p. 8; French Railways Limited, p. 9 (top);
Topham Picturepoint, p. 9 (bottom); Tony Stone Images, p. 10; Frank Spooner Pictures, p. 12;
Images Colour Library, p. 13; Paul Amos Photography, p. 14; Hong Kong Tourist Office, p. 15
(top); Zefa, p.15 (bottom); Adrian Meredith Aviation Library, p. 18; Tony Stone Images, p. 20;
Peter Russell/The Military Picture Library, p. 21 (bottom); Science Photo Library, p. 24, p.
25; Next Destination Ltd., p. 27; Britstock-IFA, p. 28

Every effort has been made to contact copyright holders of any material reproduced in
this book. Any omissions will be rectified in subsequent printings if notice is given to
the publisher.

CONTENTS

SCIENCE IN TRAVEL

How many different ways can you think of to travel from one place to another? Buses, cars, bicycles, trains, ships, and planes are all forms of transportation, and they all involve technology. Modern technology has even made it possible to travel into space.

The purpose of any form of transportation is to move people or goods from one place to another. In this book you will learn about some of the most important and some of the most recent developments in transport technology. First, however, you will find out about possibly the most important technological development of all—the wheel.

The First Wheel

Before the wheel was invented about 5,000 years ago, people moved around by boat, or they walked or rode animals. It was difficult to carry heavy loads even short distances. Wooden rollers (perhaps tree trunks) were probably the first type of wheels used to pull large objects. Some of the earliest wheeled vehicles may have been war chariots, in ancient Mesopotamia (now Iraq). Gradually the wheel spread to other parts of Asia, Africa, and Europe.

....

The first wheels were made of solid wooden planks. Spoked wheels were developed about 4,000 years ago. They were lighter, but still strong. Wheels did not change much until about 100 years ago, when they were fitted with air-filled tires, just in time for the automobile!

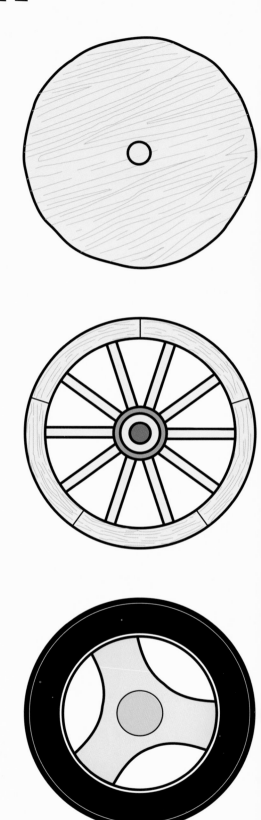

Bridges and tunnels make journeys shorter and safer. This bridge is near Seville in Spain.

Engines

Using wheels, you can pull heavier loads and travel faster with less effort than it would take by hand or by foot. For thousands of years, wheeled vehicles were pulled by animals until, less than 200 years ago, steam engines were used to power trains and ships.

Steam engines were difficult to use on the road. The invention of the **internal combustion engine** led to the development of cars and then planes. Internal combustion engines are not very efficient. They change very little of the energy in fuel into movement. Jet engines are reliable and produce more power.

Transportation technology involves much more than wheels, engines, and vehicles themselves. Roads, railroads, bridges, and tunnels are all designed and built by scientists using different kinds of materials. And, unless you can find your way by the sun and stars, you use technology to navigate. This book shows how engineers are making travel faster, safer and more efficient.

Bicycles are one of the most efficient forms of personal transportation. They became popular about 100 years ago, around the same time as the car was invented.

CARS, CARS, CARS

Henry Ford made the first car that did not cost too much to buy. Many people could then afford to go where they liked, when they liked. Today's scientists known as engineers are tackling the problems brought about by the millions of cars now speeding along our roads and polluting our streets. What are they doing to make cars safer and cleaner?

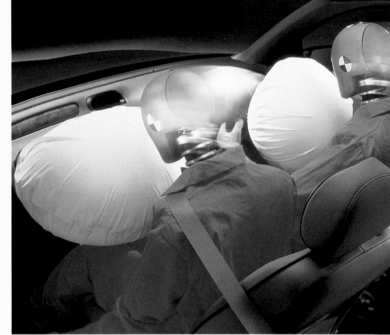

Safety

All drivers hope that their car will never be in an accident. But car designers have to prepare for the worst. Safety belts, airbags, and roll bars have helped to make driving safer.

Designers and engineers crash cars on purpose! They put dummies inside cars to see what would happen to people in different kinds of crashes.

Leaner and Cleaner

Most cars are still powered by internal combustion engines, just as the first cars were 100 years ago. Many of today's cars use fuel injection. A computer under the dashboard calculates exactly how much fuel and air should be pumped into the engine so that the fuel burns more cleanly. In modern cars, fumes are passed through devices called catalytic converters. They change the harmful gases into not so harmful substances — carbon dioxide, nitrogen, and water.

In 1908, Henry Ford began to produce the Model T Ford. By 1927 he had sold more than 15 million "Tin Lizzies," as they were called.

HOW AN INTERNAL COMBUSTION ENGINE WORKS

1. A small amount of fuel and air is sucked into the cylinder.

2. The piston moves up and squeezes the gases.

3. The fuel explodes, forcing the piston down.

4. Exhaust gases are pushed out.

A gasoline engine can have several cylinders, each with a piston. As the piston moves up, the fuel explodes and forces the piston down. As the pistons move up and down they produce the movement that turns the wheels.

Cars of the Future

Tomorrow's cars will be "intelligent." They will drive themselves on roads and help drivers to park. Road signs will beam information into the car about traffic jams on the roads ahead. A heads-up display shown in front of the driver will show the car's speed, fuel level, and the best route to follow to avoid traffic jams. The technology for all these developments has already been tried and tested.

Future cars will use new technology to make driving safer and cleaner. Satellites and computers will help drivers find the best route through traffic.

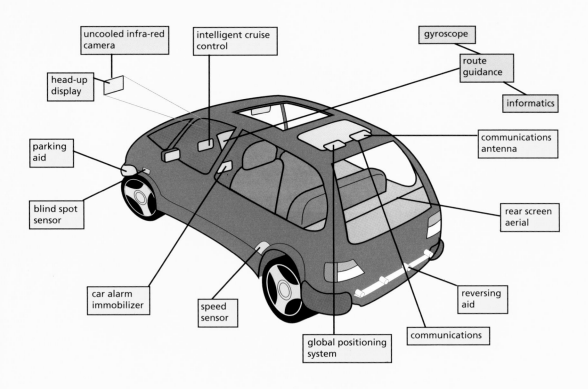

uncooled infra-red camera

intelligent cruise control

gyroscope

route guidance

head-up display

informatics

parking aid

communications antenna

blind spot sensor

rear screen aerial

car alarm immobilizer

speed sensor

reversing aid

global positioning system

communications

HIGH-SPEED TRAINS

Until the first railroads were invented, most people never traveled far from where their homes. The railroads made travel fast and cheap. They were followed by even faster airplanes, but air travel often involves long waits at airports miles from the center of cities. Many people now believe that we are at the start of a new age of their travel. Fast trains use less fuel than cars or trucks, cause less pollution, and can carry a lot more goods and people. Trains travel between major cities in one country in almost the same time as it takes by airplane. How can this be?

Fast Trains

The fastest trains in the world are all **well-designed for speed** and powered by electricity. The electric locomotive does not have to carry its fuel with it, but picks up an electric current from an overhead wire or a third rail on the track.

Eurostar

Sleek *Eurostar* passenger trains link Paris, Brussels, and London. They take just 21 minutes to pass through the Channel Tunnel, 427 feet below sea level. *Eurostar* takes only three hours to travel from the center of London to the centre of Paris. Loops of wire along the *Eurostar* track communicate with electronic equipment on board each train. This system controls the train's speed as it approaches a station and it passes signaling information directly to the driver.

Each *Eurostar* train has a specially designed locomotive, followed by 18 coaches. It is 1,300 feet long and travels at 120 miles per hour (mph). Cars and trucks are carried on special **rolling stock** on a tunnel service.

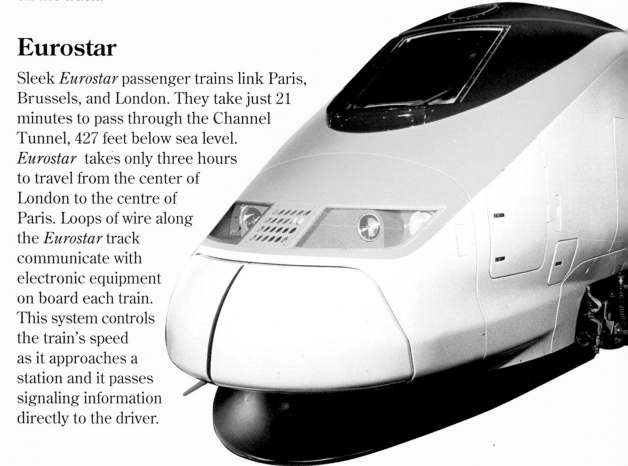

Bullet Train

The Bullet train was the first high-speed train to run on special tracks. The service began in 1964, and the trains make the 203-mile journey from Tokyo to Nagoya in Japan at more than 120 mph.

TGV

The French TGV (*Train à Grande Vitesse*) is one of the world's fastest trains. It travels at 180 mph. A powerful electric locomotive at each end drives the train along. It has eight streamlined passenger cars.

The Japanese and Germans are both developing a new kind of train that will travel faster than either the TGV or the Bullet. A maglev (short for magnetic levitation) train does not have wheels. It glides above or below the track (see page 28).

The Bullet train speeds through Japan on special tracks.

A TGV train rushes through the French countryside.

OVER, UNDER, AND THROUGH

Bridges and tunnels can make journeys safer and shorter. The longest road tunnel in the world is the St. Gotthard Tunnel in Switzerland. It is 10 miles long and saves motorists from having to drive 6,500 feet up into the mountains to cross the Alps. The extraordinary Sheto Ohashi Bridge in Japan is really six bridges in one. It links the islands of Honshu and Shilolo across the 8-mile-wide Strait of Seto. How can engineers build such huge and impressive structures?

Two Inventions

Modern bridges, such as the Houston Bridge in Texas and the Golden Gate Bridge in San Francisco, would not be possible without two 19th-century inventions: inexpensive mass-produced steel and Portland cement, from which concrete is made. Hollow concrete towers support bridges, which are then hung from strong steel cables.

The road of this suspension bridge in Houston, Texas, is suspended from long steel cables attached to tall towers near each end of the bridge. Each cable is made up of thousands of tightly bound steel wires.

SUPERBRIDGES

Suspension bridges are the longest bridges, because they use the most lightweight construction. The Golden Gate Bridge spans the entrance to the San Francisco Bay. When it was opened in 1937, it was longer (4,200 feet) and taller (746 feet) than any other bridge.

Now another suspension bridge, the River Humber Bridge in England, holds the record (4628 feet), but not for long. The Great Belt East Bridge, being built in Denmark, will be even longer. There are plans all over the world to build more superbridges.

A Precise Meeting

The railroad tunnel under the English Channel is 18.5 miles long. Work on it began in 1987, when tunnelers started digging on both the English and French coasts. Two years later, the tunnelers met under the sea, 12.5 miles from the English coast. The tunnels joined together exactly, within inches. How did the tunnelers figure out how to do this?

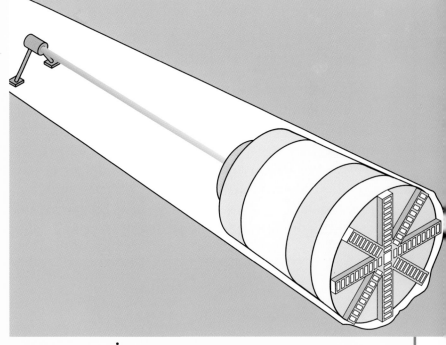

To begin, the tunnel entrances were lined up very accurately. The GPS, or Global Positioning System, was used to do this. Next, a pencil-thin laser beam was used to control the precise direction of the TBMs (tunnel-boring machines). These giant machines, which have a crew of 50 workers, grind forward at about 0.6 miles a month.

A computer-controlled "target," which is sensitive to light, is fixed to the back of a TBM. It detects the laser beam. Information from the target is fed into the TBM's computer. It allows tiny corrections to be made to the tunnelers' positions.

DELIVERING THE GOODS

The largest ships afloat today are the oil tankers that carry crude oil from oil fields to refineries. In fact most heavy cargo travels by sea. On the road, big trucks transport everything from fuel to milk and cars to fruit. Why is it that these giants of the sea and road are so efficient?

Massive Tankers

Tankers may weigh up to 500,000 tons and be 985 feet long. Their rounded bow, or front end, helps them move faster and more smoothly. Amazingly, these huge tankers are pushed through the water by a single propeller, driven by a steam turbine. (A turbine is like a propeller with many blades.) The propeller sucks in water from ahead and pushes it backward, making the ship move forward. Most ships are powered by steam or diesel engines. Marine diesel engines produce 15,000 **hp** (horsepower) and use less fuel than steam engines.

Convenient Containers

Much of the world's cargo travels in "containers"—strong, weathertight rectangular boxes. Containers are very efficient, because they are all the same size—8 feet high and wide and 19.89 or 40.01 feet long—which means they are easy to stack and to load. Containers are carried to and from the docks on railroad cars or trucks. They are lifted on and off container ships by transporter cranes. Large container ports, such as Singapore, use computers to control the arrival and departure of ships and containers.

This tanker carries oil by sea to refineries.

Travel by Truck

The bigger a truck is the more it can carry. Long-distance trucks usually have an angled panel above the cab (where the driver sits) to make them more **streamlined**. This causes air to pass smoothly over the body and so helps to reduce the amount of fuel the truck uses. Big, heavy trucks are not difficult to drive. The steering is power-assisted. When the driver turns the steering wheel, the road wheels turn easily. The system is operated by a **hydraulic** pump driven by the truck's engine.

Trucks have many wheels to carry their immense loads. Some trailers have up to 18 wheels. The tires are reinforced with steel hoops to make them stronger.

TURBO TRUCKS

Some trucks are fitted with turbochargers to make their engines more powerful. Exhaust gases from the engine drive a small gas turbine, which drives the turbocharger. This compresses the air that the engine uses to burn its fuel. This increases the efficiency of the engine. It works with sports cars, too!

FAST FERRIES

Traditional ships move fairly slowly, because the resistance of the water (the drag) pulls them back. Hydrofoils and hovercraft overcome drag by riding above the water. High-speed ferries try to compete by giving their passengers a fast, smooth ride and loading and unloading quickly. How do hydrofoils and hovercraft work? How have ferries made sailing faster and smoother?

No Tugs Needed

Car ferries with huge, watertight doors at either end are called ro-ro ferries (roll-on roll-off). Cars and trucks drive directly on and off the ship. Despite their huge size, ro-ro ferries enter and leave ports without the help of tugboats.

Ferries have powerful engines to move quickly through the water as well as bow thruster units. These consist of a reversible propeller in an underwater tunnel that stretches across the ferry near the bows. The propeller forces water to either side of the ferry, allowing the ship to turn quickly in the docks.

Some ro-ro ferries are nearly 700 feet long. They can carry more than 1,000 passengers and 800 cars.

Sea Sickness No More

People don't get sick on ferries much any more. This is because ferries, like many passenger ships, are fitted with stabilizers, which are movable, horizontal fins attached to the ship's hull. They are controlled by **gyroscopes** and help to prevent ships from rolling.

This hydrofoil can travel at speed because propellers lift it above the water and prevent water resistance from slowing the vessel down.

Large passenger hovercraft can carry more than 400 passengers and 60 cars. Four jet engines drive fans and propellers that form a cushion of air for the hovercraft to ride on.

UNDER THE SEA

Large military submarines patrol the world, hundreds of feet below the surface of the sea. They even sail under the thick ice that covers the North Pole. These amazing ships can produce their own oxygen and can stay submerged, under water, for as long as there is enough food for the crew. A **nuclear reactor** can fuel the electric motors for many years without the submarine having to surface. Smaller vessels can dive even deeper. The crews work on underwater pipelines or explore the dark ocean bed. How do submarines and submersibles dive and how do the crews find their way under the sea?

Sinking and Steering

A submarine has large tanks on either side of the hull. When the tanks fill with water, the submarine sinks lower and lower. To return to the surface, the crew blows the water out of the tanks using compressed air. The submarine then floats upward. When air is compressed it takes up only a small amount of space. When it is released, a small amount will expand to fill the tanks.

Submarines have equipment at the front and back to tilt the ship up or down. As on surface ships, rudders steer them.

This diagram shows how the tanks of either side of the submarine work. In the picture on the left, the submarine has surfaced, because there is no water in the tanks. When the submarine dives (middle), water is let in to the tanks to make the vessel heavy, so it sinks.

surfaced

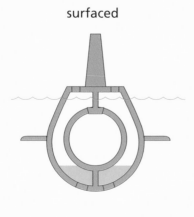

diving

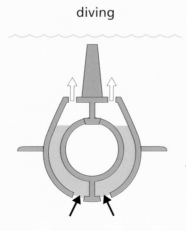

surfacing again

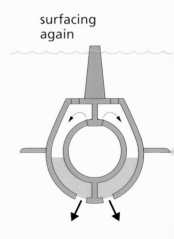

Sonar

Submarine crews use sound to help them find their way. Surface vessels searching for submarines under water also use sonar (SOund NAvigation and Ranging system). The sonar system sends out a sound signal and listens for the echo caused when the signal strikes something. The echo produces a picture of the object on a screen. The distance between the vessel and the object can be calculated from the speed of the echo.

Submersibles

Submersibles are small, specialized submarines. They are carried out to sea by a ship and used for many underwater jobs, such as repairing cables and mapping the ocean floor. They have powerful lights to help the crew see. One submersible, *Alvin*, searched for and found the *Titanic*, which sank in 1912 after hitting an iceberg.

Up Periscope

When a submarine hides just under the water, with its tower submerged, its crew can still see other ships on the surface. They look through the submarine's periscope—a device made of mirrors and lenses that sticks up above the water. The periscope can be rotated to scan all around the vessel. Video cameras also scan above and below the surface of the water.

SPEED OF SOUND

Sound travels through air at 1,086 feet per second (about one mile every five seconds). It travels through water nearly five times as fast as through air.

Submarines, are powered by diesel engines when sailing on the surface of the water. The engine needs air to burn the fuel. The air is sucked in through a tube in the tower on the top of the ship.

FLYING HIGH

The fastest way for most of us to travel is by airplane. Airliners can carry up to 400 passengers at a time and get them from place to place at 600 mph. *Concorde* travels even faster. It can carry 139 passengers from Paris to New York in just 3.5 hours. Many people are frightened of flying, yet it is the safest form of transportation. How have engineers made flying so safe? Why can *Concorde* fly so fast?

Fastest Passenger Plane

Concorde is the fastest airliner in the world. It flies at 1,380 mph, nearly twice as fast as the speed of sound. It can fly this fast because it has extra powerful engines and its swept-back wings and long, thin body make it more streamlined than other airplanes.

Autopilot

Air travel is very safe, because the aircraft is controlled mainly by computer. The aircraft's route is planned by air traffic control. The pilot inputs the direction, speed, and height to the aircraft's computer and, once the wheels have left the runway, switches over to autopilot. From then on the airplane's computer controls the aircraft. The pilots watch the instruments and can always take over from the autopilot in an emergency.

Concorde's long, smooth, thin shape makes it easy for it to cut through the air without **friction**.

Super Heat

The air friction caused by flying at superhigh speeds creates immense heat. *Concorde* is built from titanium, a metal that is expensive but more resistant to heat than aluminum **alloys** used in slower aircraft.

WHAT MAKES AN AIRCRAFT FLY?

How does a 300-ton aircraft become a graceful flying machine? The answer lies in the shape of its wings.

As a wing cuts through the air, air is forced over the upper and lower surfaces of the wing. While the underside of the wing is nearly flat, the upper side is highly curved. Air has to travel farther over the top of the wing than underneath it. This "stretches" the air, making it less dense. As a result, the air pressure is higher under the wing than above it. The air under the wing "pushes up" to provide the lift that keeps the aircraft in the air.

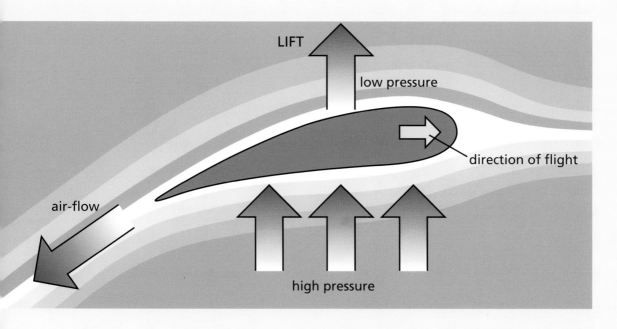

LIFT
low pressure
direction of flight
air-flow
high pressure

STRAIGHT UP

What do hot-air balloons, jump jets, helicopters, and airships have in common? They can all hover, or fly in one position, above the earth, without moving forward or backward. Hot-air balloons and airships float because they are lighter than air. Jump jets and helicopters, however, are heavier than air. They have to keep "pushing" to stay up. How can helicopters do this, and why are balloons and airships lighter than air?

Floating

When you swim, you float. This is because the same amount of water as you weighs more than you do. This difference in weight gives you **buoyancy**, which was first explained by **Archimedes**. Hot-air balloons "float" in the sky because hot air weighs less than the cold air that surrounds the balloon. In the past, airships were filled with hydrogen gas, which weighs much less than air. So the airships floated, too.

DEW POWER?

Cyrano de Bergerac (1619–1655), the French writer, noticed how morning dew rises off the ground in the heat of the sun's rays. De Bergerac suggested building an aircraft shaped like a huge glass ball, containing dew. When warmed by the sun, the dew inside would rise and take the aircraft with it. Cyrano proposed voyages to other planets, as well as flights on earth.

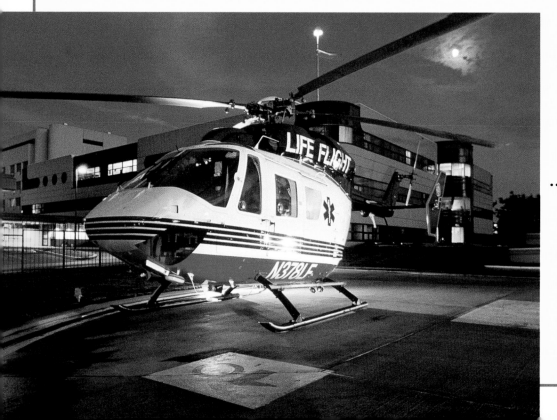

Helicopters are often used to rescue people in an emergency. They can take off and land in a small area.

Helicopters

Helicopters can fly straight up, forward, backward, or hover in one place. The long, thin rotor blades lift the helicopter and move it along. They are attached to a jet engine and, as the blades spin around, they pull the helicopter up into the air. The pilot changes the angle of the blades to change direction.

Balloons

The first hot-air balloon was made of paper and flew in 1753. A modern balloon is strong but light. It is made from nylon and coated with a kind of plastic. Hot air from a gas burner fills the balloon. Propane gas is stored as a liquid in containers inside the basket. The pilot controls the height byblasting hot air into the balloon.

Jump Jets

Like a helicopter, a jump jet can take off from a small space, such as the roof of a building. The exhaust gas from the engine is directed downward through four swiveling nozzles. This provides the lift. Once in the air, the nozzles swing back, and the jump jet flies forward like an ordinary aircraft.

A balloon drifts above the countryside. The pilot controls the height by adjusting the gas burner.

The Hawker-Siddely Harrier jump jet does not need a runway to take off and land.

JET REVOLUTION

Most high-speed aircraft are driven by jet engines. So are helicopters, naval ships, and even power stations that make electricity. An experimental car has been designed with a jet engine. And one day we may even have our own jet packs for getting quickly from place to place. How do jet engines work?

Jet engines are reliable and produce more power than most other engines of the same size. A jet engine of an aircraft is basically a tube that sucks in air at one end and uses it to burn fuel. It produces a stream of red-hot exhaust gases, which blasts backward and thrusts the engine (and the aircraft) forward. Jet engines get very hot, so they are made of special alloys that do not melt. There are three main types of jet engine: the turbojet, the turboprop, and the turbofan.

The Turbojet

A turbojet has a turbine inside the engine. The turbine is spun by the stream of exhaust gases passing through it. The turbine **compresses** the air and pushes it through the engine more quickly.

Turbojets are noisy but small. Many military airplanes use them, because they can easily be given more power.

Turbojets are the simplest kind of jet engine. They work by pushing a jet of hot air out of the plane. This hits the air so fast that the reaction thrusts the plane forward.

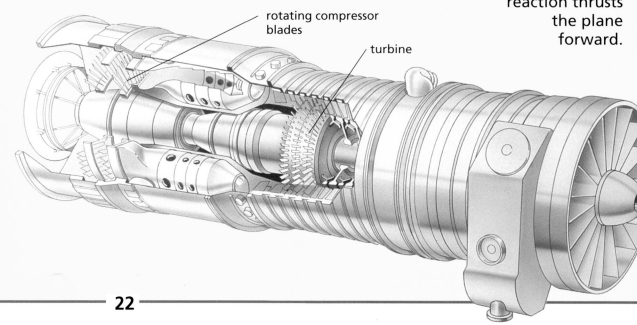

rotating compressor blades

turbine

The Turboprop

The turbine in a turboprop engine is used to drive a propeller as well as a compressor. The propeller drives the plane forward. The hot exhaust gases also produce some thrust, as in a turbojet. Turbojets are slower than pure jets, but they do not use as much fuel.

The Turbofan

A turbofan engine has an enormous fan at the front that sucks in huge amounts of air. Most of the air bypasses the turbine and joins the exhaust gases, to give more thrust.

Turbofans are the best kind of jet engine for a passenger aircraft. They are quieter than turbojets and use less fuel. Nevertheless a jumbo jet may use 52,800 gallons of fuel on a single flight from the United States to Europe. The fuel is stored in large tanks in the aircraft's wings.

Although personal jet packs may seem an unlikely method of transport and are currently used only by the Army, maybe one day we will all use them to get around quickly!

NEWTON'S REACTION

Every action produces an equal but opposite reaction.

According to this famous law of motion, first stated by English scientist Sir Isaac Newton (1642– 1727), the forward motion of a jet aircraft is a result of reaction. The exhaust gases shooting back in the jet engine provide the action. The reaction is the thrust that propels the aircraft forward.

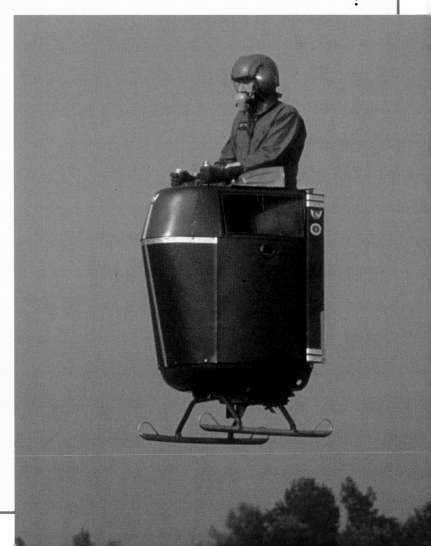

SPACE TRAVEL

We have scarcely begun to explore the vast distances and billions of stars that make up the universe. For hundreds of years, astronomers have studied the stars from earth. But it was only 40 years ago that the first spacecraft was launched. Since then unpiloted aircraft called probes have explored many of the planets. Today astronauts regularly shuttle backward and forward to space laboratories. How can space probes travel such huge distances? What do astronauts do out there in space?

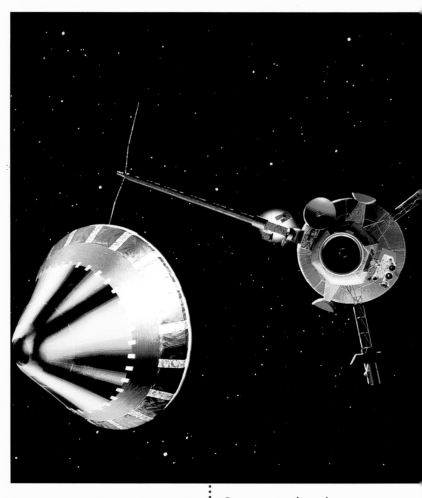

Slingshots in Space

Since 1962, unpiloted probes have flown past every planet except Pluto. They are launched into space at the fantastic speed of 24,000 miles per hour. They also use the pull of **gravity** of the planets they visit to boost their speed. First the gravity of the planet pulls them in, and they gain speed. Then their speed becomes so great that they are flung out into space, with great force, on a new course. Even so, their journey can take several years.

The instruments on a probe need electricity. Those that explore the inner planets use **solar power** but those, such as *Galileo*, that travel to the outer planets, use special batteries instead.

Space probes have explored the **solar system**—the sun and the nine planets that orbit it. In 1995 *Galileo* traveled more than 85,000 miles to the planet Jupiter. The journey took five months. Once there *Galileo* released a special probe to measure Jupiter's atmosphere. *Galileo* went on to explore Jupiter's many moons for two more years.

Hubble Telescope

Probes send us photographs of the planets by radio. But to see beyond the planets to other stars and galaxies we have to rely on telescopes. Radio telescopes on earth can pick up radio waves from stars billions of miles away, but the radio signals have to pass through the blanket of the earth's atmosphere. In 1990 the Hubble telescope was launched into orbit around the earth. It is now picking up and sending back much clearer information than telescopes on earth. For example, astronomers now have evidence of planets circling around other stars.

The Space Shuttle

The Hubble telescope could not have been launched without the help of the Space Shuttle. This re-usable spacecraft was first launched in 1981. It carries astronauts, satellites, and equipment into orbit around the earth. Since its launch, some of the clearest pictures ever of deep space have been beamed back to earth.

The space shuttle *Discovery* takes off into space.

LIGHT YEAR

A light year is a unit of length. It is equal to the distance that light travels in one year in a vacuum, or about 5.88 trillion miles.

FINDING THE WAY

Years ago, people explored the world using only compasses and other simple instruments to find their way. The magnet in a compass always points toward the earth's magnetic north. Compasses on steel ships or airplanes can be affected by the metal of the ship and have to be protected. However, this protected type of compass does not work on a spacecraft. How do compasses work? What do modern ships, airplanes, and spacecraft use to find their way?

Triangulation

The magnetized needle in a compass always points north, toward the earth's **magnetic pole**. So you can use a compass to find the bearing, or direction, of any object. If you find the bearings of two objects and draw them on a map, then your position is shown by the point where the lines cross.

Radio Beacons

Ships and aircraft use radio signals to calculate their exact position. This is the same method as triangulation with a compass, except that the bearings are calculated from the direction of the signals picked up by a receiver on the ship or airplane. The advantage of using radio signals is that they can be picked up at night or in fog.

Gyrocompasses

Magnetic compasses are difficult to use on large ships, because the needle is affected by steel and iron. A **gyrocompass** is used instead. This compass consists of an electric gyroscope. Once spinning, the gyroscope's **axis** always points in the same direction, and in the same direction as the earth's axis. This causes the gyroscope's axis to point north. Spacecraft also use gyrocompasses to give them a fixed direction to steer by when out of reach of the earth's magnetic field.

This man wants to find out where he is. He is taking the bearings of two objects near him. If he then marks the bearings on a map, the point where the two lines meet is his position.

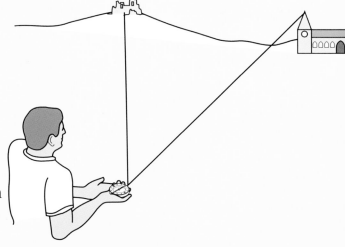

Steering by Satellite

The Global Positioning System (GPS) uses 24 **satellites** orbiting in fixed positions above the Earth. The satellites send out radio signals, which are picked up by special receivers on earth. A computer inside the receiver then works out its exact position to within a few inches. Anyone can buy a special receiver and use GPS to figure out where he or she is.

GPS was first designed for the U.S. Army, Air Force, and Navy. Now aircraft and ships use it, too. In the future, cars and other forms of transportation will probably be fitted with receivers linked to GPS. Already some bus companies, security firms, and other organizations use GPS to tell them exactly where all their vehicles are. Each vehicle has a receiver fitted to its roof.

Easy-to-use handheld receivers allow hikers to use the Global Positioning System.

TRAVEL IN THE FUTURE

Wat will the future really hold? Will we travel about on jet packs, or will there be an entirely new form of super-fast transportation, like that portrayed in science-fiction movies? Entirely new technology is difficult to predict, but one thing is certain: transportation will have to cause less pollution. Maglev trains that use superconductors need very little electricity and offer a smooth, fast ride. How do they work, and what other sources of fuel might we be using in the future?

Magnetic Trains

The smoothest trains have no wheels and are known as Maglev trains. *Maglev* is short for magnetic levitation, a system that uses powerful **electromagnets** to lift the train a few inches above or below the track. Other magnets propel and guide the train. Experimental Maglev trains have already been developed in Germany and Japan, and in Britain a Maglev train carries people from the railway station to the airport.

Maglev trains do not have to overcome **friction** between the track and the train, and so they can travel very fast. In Japan one train carrying passengers reached a record 240.5 miles per hour along a 4-mile experimental track. In Germany the Maglev Transrapid has traveled as fast as 247.5 miles per hour.

This German overhead Maglev train uses very little electricity and creates less pollution than other trains.

Superconductors

Superconducting magnets could make Maglev travel very efficient. A **superconductor** loses all electrical resistance at very low temperatures, so electromagnets using it need very little electricity. The race is on to find a material that superconducts at ordinary temperatures.

New Fuels

Diesel and gasoline are both made from oil. One day oil supplies will run out. Manufacturers are looking for new sources of fuel. One possibility is vegetable oil, made from sunflower oil, or sugar. Already the Brazilians have made gasoline from sugar cane, which, unlike oil, can be replanted and will not run out. Burning fuel made from sugar or vegetable oil releases the carbon dioxide that was used when the plant grew (probably the year before). Burning fossil fuels release carbon dioxide that was trapped millions of years ago. Release of carbon dioxide into the atmosphere causes problems for the environment.

A new fuel is being tested that is almost pollution-free. A fuel cell is a kind of battery that burns hydrogen to produce water and electricity. Fuel cells are almost 100 percent efficient, which means they use almost all the energy obtained from burning hydrogen. This is much more efficient than gasoline engines.

GLOBAL WARMING

Burning fossil fuels increases the amount of carbon dioxide in the atmosphere. This acts like a blanket over the earth and traps heat. If this happens too often, the earth's temperature will rise, causing many problems.

This bus in Vancouver, Canada, gets its energy from a fuel cell.

GLOSSARY

alloy a material that consists of two or more metals

Archimedes a famous ancient Greek mathematician, born about 287 BC. He founded the science of hydrostatics, which deals with floating objects.

axis buoyancy the upward thrust on an object that is immersed in a liquid. Archimedes discovered that the thrust is equal to the weight of the liquid displaced by the object.

compress squash air, increasing its pressure

electromagnet a kind of magnet made of iron. It only becomes magnetic when an electric current flows in the coil of wire wrapped around it.

friction when two surfaces rub together, friction is the force that slows their movement and produces heat. Oil and grease are used to reduce the friction between the moving parts of an engine or the wheel bearings on a vehicle.

gravity the force experienced by any object that has mass and is near the earth. It causes objects thrown in the air to fall back down to the ground. The force of gravity exists on other planets and moons and depends on their mass and diameter.

gyroscope a spinning disc with a heavy rim. When it is set in any position, it resists any change of direction. As gyroscopes have this property they are used inside gyrocompasses.

hp (horsepower) this is used to measure the power of engines. It was originally used to compare the power of steam engines to the power of horses.

hydraulic hydraulics is the science of moving liquids through pipes. The hydraulic brakes of a vehicle work by transmitting forces through liquids in pipes.

internal combustion engine any engine in which the fuel is burned in combustion chambers inside the engine. Examples are gasoline engines and diesel engines. In contrast, the fuel for a steam engine is burned in a separate furnace.

magnetic pole the region of a magnet from where its magnetic force appears to start. A bar magnet has a north pole at one end and a south pole at the other. The earth has two magnetic poles.

nuclear reactor a nuclear reactor produces heat by splitting atoms of the chemical uranium in a controlled situation. The heat produced can be used to generate electricity.

satellite any small body that orbits around a much bigger one. The moon is a natural satellite of the earth; communications satellites for radio and television, and navigational satellites are artificial ones.

solar power power obtained from the energy of the Sun's rays. The sun gives light and heat. The heat can be used directly. The light can be changed into electricity by solar panels.

solar system all the planets in orbit around the Sun. It also includes all the comets, asteroids, and meteors.

streamlined a streamlined shape moves easily through a fluid, such as water or air. There is very little friction between the outside of the object and the fluid. The streamlined object offers little resistance, or drag.

superconductor a material that allows electricity to flow through it at very low temperatures without resistance (loss of energy). Ordinary conductors resist the flow of electricity.

FACT FILE

- The deepest dive ever made by a manned submersible took place on January 23, 1960. The bathyscaphe *Trieste* descended 35,826 feet into the Challenger Deep in the Pacific Ocean's Marianas Trench.

- The exploration of space began on October 4, 1957, when the first satellite, *Sputnik 1*, was launched by the Russians. Two years later, a Russian spacecraft took the first pictures of the far side of the moon, which always faces away from earth.

- The *Graf Zeppelin* (the first aircraft to travel around the world) made more than 500 transatlantic crossings.

- Between 1900 and 1939, 52,000 people traveled 1.2 million miles by airship.

- The British *de Havilland Comet* was, in 1949, the first commercial jet airliner.

- Dick Rutan and Jeana Yeager flew non-stop around the world in 1986 in nine days. Their lightweight aircraft, *Voyager*, had twin engines and weighed 1,984 pounds with its cargo. With all the fuel needed for its non-stop trip, it weighed 9,283 pounds!

- The first underground railroad ran in London in 1863. It was 3.9 miles long and used a steam locomotive.

FURTHER READINGS

Ardely, Neil. *The Science Book of Motion*. Harcourt, 1992.

Barrett, Norman. *Space Machines*. Franklin Watts, 1994.

Dunn, Andrew. *Wheels at Work*. Thomson Learning, 1993.

Graham, Ian. *Boats, Ships, Submarines, and Other Floating Machines.* Kingfisher Books, 1993.

Oxlade, Chris. *Bridges and Tunnels*. Franklin Watts, 1994.

INDEX